IMAGES OF ENGLAND

Around
Newton Abbot

St Leonard's Tower, known locally as 'The Clock Tower', has often been the focal point of Newton Abbot's civic past. Never more so than in 1688, when William of Orange's declaration was read out to people of Newton Abbot and Kingsteignton. William, on his way to London to begin a joint reign with his wife Mary II as William III, promised to uphold the 'Liberties of England and the Protestant Religion...' Here an enormous crowd has gathered on 8 February 1952 to listen to the proclamation of Elizabeth II read by the chairman of the Urban District Council, Joseph James George. The proclamation, signed by all councillors, can be seen on page 6. The Tower originally had a small chapel attached (it is mentioned as early as 1350) but it was demolished in 1836 leaving only the tower. A new St Leonard's chapel was built in Wolborough Street, its foundation stone being laid on 20 September 1834 by Mr Thomas Knight Sweetland, the oldest Feoffee at the time. The retention of the tower on its old site, plus the fact that the new St Leonard's has no tower, leads to the saying that Newton Abbot 'has a tower without a church and a church without a tower'.

IMAGES OF ENGLAND

Around
Newton Abbot

Les Berry and Gerald Gosling

NONSUCH

First published 1994
This new pocket edition 2005
Images unchanged from first edition

Nonsuch Publishing Limited
The Mill, Brimscombe Port,
Stroud, Gloucestershire, GL5 2QG
www.nonsuch-publishing.com

British Library Cataloguing in Publication Data.
A catalogue record for this book is available from the British Library.

ISBN 1-84588-163-X

Typesetting and origination by Nonsuch Publishing Limited
Printed in Great Britain by Oaklands Book Services Limited

Contents

THE PROCLAMATION

WHEREAS IT HAS PLEASED ALMIGHTY GOD TO CALL TO HIS MERCY OUR LATE SOVEREIGN LORD KING GEORGE VI, OF BLESSED AND GLORIOUS MEMORY, BY WHOSE DECEASE THE CROWN IS SOLELY AND RIGHTFULLY COME TO THE HIGH AND MIGHTY PRINCESS ELIZABETH ALEXANDRA MARY:

"WE, THEREFORE, THE LORDS SPIRITUAL AND TEMPORAL OF THIS REALM, BEING HERE ASSISTED WITH THESE OF HER LATE MAJESTY'S PRIVY COUNCIL, WITH REPRESENTATIVES OF OTHER MEMBERS OF THE COMMONWEALTH, WITH OTHER PRINCIPAL GENTLEMEN OF QUALITY, WITH THE LORD MAYOR, ALDERMEN, AND CITIZENS OF LONDON, DO NOW HEREBY WITH ONE VOICE AND CONSENT OF TONGUE AND HEART PUBLISH AND PROCLAIM THAT THE HIGH AND MIGHTY PRINCESS ELIZABETH ALEXANDRA MARY IS NOW, BY THE DEATH OF OUR LATE SOVEREIGN OF HAPPY MEMORY, BECOME QUEEN ELIZABETH II BY THE GRACE OF GOD, QUEEN OF THIS REALM, AND OF HER OTHER REALMS AND TERRITORIES, HEAD OF THE COMMONWEALTH, DEFENDER OF THE FAITH, TO WHOM HER LIEGES DO ACKNOWLEDGE ALL FAITH AND CONSTANT OBEDIENCE WITH HEARTY AND HUMBLE AFFECTION, BESEECHING GOD BY WHOM KINGS AND QUEENS DO REIGN TO BLESS THE ROYAL PRINCESS, ELIZABETH II, WITH LONG AND HAPPY YEARS TO REIGN OVER US.

GOD SAVE THE QUEEN

Introduction

Newton Abbot lies between the moors and the sea, at the head of the Teign estuary, and has been inhabited since the first century BC. Bronze artifacts were excavated from Milber Down fort in the 1930s.

At the beginning of the thirteenth century the two expanding communities of Teignwick (Highweek) and Wolborough, divided by the River Lemon, held markets and fairs: Highweek on All Saints Day and Ascension Day, together with a weekly market, and Wolborough in honour of St Leonard on 5, 6 and 7 November, the chief attraction on these dates being the Cheese and Onion fair.

Wolborough Manor had become Torre Abbey's richest possession by the end of the thirteenth century. Theobald de Englishville left his manor of Teignwick to his nephew in 1262, passing to his son Theobald Bushel in 1269. The 'new' towns, became known as Newton Abbot (of the Abbots of Torre) and Newton Bushel. They finally merged at the turn of the nineteenth century.

Robert Bushel built the Manor House at Bradley. In 1402 the manor passed through the female line to the Yarde family.

Richard Yarde was appointed Sheriff of Devon in 1442. A new church was built at Highweek in 1428, and with the their new found wealth the Yardes built the north aisle at Highweek and added an impressive window to the chapel of St Mary's in Newton Bushel. The Yarde window was moved to St Mary's Abbotsbury in 1904 to serve as the east window when 'old' St Mary's became derelict.

In 1545 the king sold the manor of Wolborough to John Gaverock, who was the steward for the Abbot at Torre; he built a new manorial home at Forde. By 1610 Sir Richard Reynell had acquired Forde, and expanded the building to its present state, incorporating many fine plaster ceilings and ornamentation in the house. Forde House entertained two kings – Charles I and his court stayed there in 1625, on his way to and from inspecting his fleet in Plymouth.

In 1688 Prince William of Orange brought fame to Newton Abbot by proclaiming his intention to be king for the first time. The declaration was read to the public from St Leonard's Tower in Wolborough Street. He proceeded to Forde House and was lavishly entertained by Sir William Courtenay's household, as Sir William, although courteous, was not present for political reasons.

Newton Abbot and Newton Bushel both prospered from the wool and leather industries that built up in the middle ages, together with the clay and pottery industries. In the seventeenth to nineteenth centuries the link with Newfoundland and the cod fisheries had an enormous influence on Newton Abbot. Ships used to sail from Newton Abbot to Newfoundland. Holbeam Mill supplied fish hooks and knives, and many industries thrived on this particular trade, including boot and shoemakers. Many traders received fish as payment.

Prosperity was brought to Newton Abbot in 1846 when the South Devon Railway, designed by Brunel, reached the town. History might have been otherwise as Ashburton was also considered to be a suitable site; luckily Newton Abbot was chosen.

The town became a major rail centre, with extensive repair sheds and marshalling yards, and at the turn of the century the railway was one of the town's biggest employers.

Newton Abbot has a varied and remarkable history, much of which has not even been touched upon in this introduction. With the publishing of this book, fascinating glimpses of the past can be seen. To some it will bring back fond memories; others will have their eyes opened to the wealth of interest that was, and is, Newton Abbot.

Felicity Cole
Town & Great Western Railway Museum
2a St Paul's Road, Newton Abbot
1994

Telephone No. 86

H. & S. BEARE,
Furnishing and General Ironmongers.

IRONMONGERS, PLUMBERS & RANGE FITTERS.

SCALES, WEIGHTS, CYCLES, GUNS, PUMPS, FENCING AND GENERAL PLUMBING DONE BY EXPERIENCED WORKMEN.   CYCLE AND MOTOR AGENTS.

30, Queen St., NEWTON ABBOT.

One

The Town

The old Exeter Road Almshouses, Newton Abbot, which were demolished in 1978. Originally a lepers' hospital stood on this site.

Left: Workmen placing the figure of 'Freedom' on the plinth of the War Memorial in Devon Square, Newton Abbot, shortly before its unveiling in 1922.

Below: Although this card is marked 'The Avenue, Newton Abbot', it is in fact a view looking down St Paul's Road towards the War Memorial in around 1931. The Avenue is the street seen in the background behind the War Memorial.

THE AVENUE NEWTON ABBOT.

IG483

Devon Square and Queen Street, Newton Abbot, *c.* 1901. Modern-day conservationists would not be too annoyed at the thought of the magnificent oak being felled, which it was in around 1920, because the timber was sold and the money went towards the cost of the war memorial which was erected in the Square.

The Clock Tower and the Globe Hotel, Courtenay Street, Newton Abbot, c. 1945. Both the Globe and Stiling's chemists shop opposite are now part of Austin's departmental store, which is sad – the Globe, an old coaching inn, had been elegantly modernised throughout and was one of the area's top hotels, its Buttery and Oyster Bar being especially popular.

Opposite above: Wolborough Street and the Clock Tower, c. 1956.

Opposite below: Unveiling of the World War Two addition to the War Memorial by Earl Fortescue CB, OBE, MC, JP, Lord Lieutenant of the County of Devon, 21 June 1949.

Wolborough Street, showing
the Clock Tower.

WRECK OF THE CONSTITUTIONAL CLUB 1908

Riot at the Constitutional (Conservative) Club in Union Street, 18 January 1908. The town was in the Liberal-held Mid-Devon (Ashburton) constituency when a by-election was called following the elevation of the sitting member, H.T. Eve, to the High Court Bench. The Suffragete Mrs Pankhurst and her daughter canvassed for the Conservative candidate, a Captain Morrison Bell who later stood for Honiton. He won a surprise victory, whereupon the Liberal supporters attacked Mrs Pankhurst and her friends and, when they had reached a place of safety, turned their attentions on the Constitutional Club.

Newton Abbot Market, c. 1928. Mention of a market at Newton Abbot is made as far back as 1220, when the Abbots of Torre held a weekly market. According to Donald McNee Stirling (1830), 'Soon after Sir William Waller came to reside at Ford, he attempted to wrest the market of Newton-Abbot from the Yardes, of Bradley; but although Sir William was a brave general in the field of Mars, he experienced a woeful defeat in the court of King's Bench; of which in his recollections, he thus pathetically says, "my endeavours to supplant Mr Yarde in his possession of the market at Newton-Abbot, though upon a dormant title, yet proceeding from a covetous end, was justly punished by loss of the thing sued for, and in all that befell me in the King's Bench."' Stirling left soon after writing his book on General Outlines of Newton and Its Vicinity and became headmaster of Colyton Grammar School (1834–63), where he died in office and was buried in St George's burial ground in Colyton.

Newton Abbot Market in the early 1920s, with Halcyon Road in the background.

Newton Abbot Market, c. 1954.

WM. BADCOCK & SONS

LIMITED

Drapers, Tailors, Outfitters,
HOUSE FURNISHERS AND REMOVAL CONTRACTORS.

Agents for **DR. JAEGER** and **CELLULAR UNDERCLOTHING.**

Price Lists and Estimates Free.   *All Parcels sent Carriage Paid.*

NEWTON ABBOT

Willliam Badcock & Sons Ltd, the Courtenay Street furnishers, shown here from a 1910 advertisment, was one of Newton Abbot's leading businesses at the time.

The Shaldon and St Marychurch Roads, c. 1925.

Three generations of the Newton Abbot boot-making family, the Fords, seen here at the shop at the corner of Halcyon and Highweek Streets. Left to right: Dorothy Cross (grand-daughter), George Ford, Florrie Ford, his daughter. The premises are now the St Mary's Court warden-controlled flats.

Queen Street, Newton Abbot, c. 1903.

Queen Street, Newton Abbot, c. 1932.

Queen Street, Newton Abbot, c. 1903. W. Brown's book shop is now a take-away.

Queen Street, Newton Abbot, c. 1908. Bartlett's Chocolate Shop on the left is now the post office.

Madge Mellor's was a prominent feature of Newton Abbot's commercial life ever since Mr and Mrs Robert Ashworth moved from Southport in 1928 to open their confectionery business, family bakery and shop in Queen Street. The business, seen right in around 1937, finally closed in 1987. After 1937 the next-door premises belonging to the fruiterers Milford's was bought, and in 1940 further expansion took place when the butchers shop on the other side was acquired but almost immediately requisitioned by the Army. The entire shop front was rebuilt in 1959. Morning coffee and afternoon teas were served in the restaurant downstairs; above were the kitchens and bakery with its massive ovens.

Mr and Mrs Robert Ashworth with their Madge Mellor's staff on the roof of their Queen Street premises.

Queen Street, c. 1932, with W.H. Smith and Madge Mellor's on the right.

East Street, Newton Abbot, *c.* 1903.

The old Commercial Hotel in Queen Street, Newton Abbot, *c.* 1908.

Left: St Leonard's Tower, Newton Abbot, 1905.

Below: World War Two bomb damage in Mount Pleasant Road, c. 1942.

Ashburton Road and the Broadlands council housing estate, Newton Abbot, in the 1930s.

Courtenay Street, Newton Abbot, *c.* 1904. White's Penny Bazaar on the right closed after the arrival next door of Marks & Spencers. Now it is part of Austins Stores.

"FORDE HOUSE,"

Within five minutes walk of the Railway Station.

NEWTON ABBOT, SOUTH DEVON.

A CATALOGUE

OF THE SALE TO BE HELD AT

The above Historical Mansion, the property of the late
W. J. WATTS, Esq., J.P., D.L., on
MONDAY, TUESDAY, WEDNESDAY, THURSDAY, FRIDAY, SATURDAY & MONDAY,
the 15th, 16th, 17th, 18th, 19th, 20th, and 22nd days of May, 1905.

CATALOGUES 1/- EACH.

MR. JAMES STOOKE, F.S.I.,
Auctioneer,
Newton Abbot.

Forde House, 22 May 1905. Originally built around 1540, Forde House was extended in 1610 by Sir Richard Reynell. Contrasting visitors were Charles I (1625) and, during the Civil War (1646), both Oliver Cromwell and Sir Thomas Fairfax. It also played host to William of Orange in 1688 shortly after he landed at Brixham. Forde belonged to the Courtenay family for around 250 years, hence Courtenay Park and Street and Powderham Road in the town. In 1979 the house and grounds were acquired by Teignbridge District Council; it is used today as their administrative HQ.

Courtenay Street, Newton Abbot, c. 1901.

Courtenay Street, Newton Abbot, during the 1891 blizzard.

LOOMAN BAWDON'S

FOR

General & Furnishing Drapery,

MILLINERY & DRESSMAKING.

A STOREHOUSE OF ART NEEDLEWORK,

Berlin and Paton Knitting Wools,

IN A GREAT VARIETY.

Pearsall's Knitting and Crochet Silks in all Shades
and Makes.

28, Courtenay St., Newton Abbot.

Looman Bawdon's General and Furnishing Drapery shop at 28 Courtenay Street, Newton
Abbot, at the turn of the century. As they claim below the shop's name, this was 'the
noted house for all needlework'. They also claimed to be 'a storehouse of art needlework',
stocking Berlin and Paton knitting wools and Pearsall's knitting and crochet silks in 'all
shades and makes'.

The River Teign and the Kingsteignton Road from Knowles Hill, Newton Abbot, in around 1908. Note the almost complete lack of development in the area.

Middleton's Glass and China Stores in Queen Street, Newton Abbot, c. 1901.

Newton Abbot Town Hall in Courtenay Street, decorated for the 1935 Silver Jubilee of King George V.

Celebrations at Market Street (Sherborne Road) Post Office, Newton Abbot, for Queen Victoria's Diamond Jubilee (1897). Note the postmen's bicycles among the decorations. The town's permanent memorial took the form of an endowment of the Newton Hospital, over £1,000 being raised, but there were more convivial celebrations. As many as 2,000 children had tea in the market, followed by games and maypole dancing in the Park. The ill were not forgotten: 109 sick people had a meal delivered to them. A later party in the market was for 600 children and 900 adults. Of special interest was an illuminated bicycle procession on Wolborough Hill. Finally, after a ball in the Alexandra Hotel, the bill for the celebrations came to £245 15s. 6d.

Newton Abbot from Powderham Park, c. 1914.

Tree Planting in Courtenay Park on Edward VII's Coronation Day in 1903. The day's proceedings opened with a short service in St Leonard's Church. Then the children marched to the Park where four of them planted the two oak trees which had been given by Dr R.H. Grimbly. Later 2,000 children had tea and each was given a box of chocolate. A giant bonfire on Wolborough Hill, Newton Abbot's traditional spot for same, rounded off the day.

Wolborough Street, Newton Abbot, *c.* 1955. The handsome and popular Half Moon Inn, the Royal Oak, its immediate right-hand neighbour, and both the premises to its left, were demolished and are now the road and roundabout leading to a car park.

Opposite above: Courtenay Park, Newton Abbot, *c.* 1910. The park, one of Newton Abbot's prized assets, was laid out in 1854 on land belonging to the Earl of Devon.

Opposite below: Courtenay Park, Newton Abbot, *c.* 1905. St Paul's church is just visible on the skyline.

Floods in Market Street, c. 1930.

Newton Abbot Market during floods, c. 1930.

The Queen's Hotel, Newton Abbot, c. 1902. Situated as it was opposite the station, the Queen's catered for the railway trade, but by 1952, when it was still advertising as being 'Family and Commercial', it proudly boasted being 'The ideal centre for Dartmoor and all resorts on the South Devon Coast'.

Bank St., Newton Abbot.

Bank Street, Newton Abbot, *c.* 1904. Scott's store, in the centre background (the area known locally as Fosse Corner), has been demolished. Formerly called Bridge Street, Bank Street took its name from the banks that set up there. Happily, even without any banks today, it retains its Bank Street name.

Newton Abbot, Free Library & Technical School.

The Free Library and Technical School, Newton Abbot, *c.* 1908. The library was the gift of John Passmore Edwards (1823–1911), a Cornishman from Blackwater near Truro. His connection with Newton Abbot was through his mother, who was a native of the town and lived in East Street. He became a journalist and founded a huge publishing empire. Later in life he financed as many as seventy-two institutions including twenty-three Free Libraries. Outside of his publishing activities he contested Truro (1868) as an Independent and was successful at Salisbury (1880) in becoming an MP. But he was not entirely happy with a political life. He twice declined a knighthood.

Left: Sutton's Dairy, Wolborough Street, Newton Abbot, *c.* 1930. Mr Sutton is standing in front.

Below: Union Street, Newton Abbot, *c.* 1925.

Lloyd's Bank, Courtenay Street, Newton Abbot, *c.* 1901.

Sherborne Road, Newton Abbot, *c.* 1900, now a car park.

Courtenay Street, Newton Abbot, *c.* 1905. The Drum Clock on Lloyd's Bank, so-called because of its shape, is still a popular Newton Abbot landmark. Frank Lawes Clothing Mart (motto: 'Always Something New, Immense Stock') stood at the junction of Courtenay Street and Market Street. It lost the buildings to the rear (right) when a service road was made for the premises on that side of the street. The Methodist church in the background was replaced by Woolworths which, in turn, has also gone.

Kingskerswell Road, Decoy, Newton Abbot, c. 1905.

Decoy, Newton Abbot, c. 1906.

The Cattle Market, Newton Abbot, *c.* 1907.

Wolborough Street, Newton Abbot, *c.* 1952. Once the older part of the town, where the market was held, today all this has gone to make way for a car park.

79774. NEWTON ABBOT, GREAT WESTERN STATION.

Newton Abbot railway station, 1935. The railway reached Newton Abbot towards the end of 1846, and shortly afterwards (1847) Isambard Kingdom Brunel talked the South Devon Railway Company into switching from steam to the atmospheric method. Trains using this method did not need a locomotive for hauling power; instead a flat-topped wagon called a piston was used. A cast-iron pipe around 15 inches in diameter was laid between the rails inside which a piston travelled. Pumping stations were built at about three-mile intervals; they exhausted the air in front of the piston so that the atmospheric pressure behind pushed it forward. When a train was due the pumping stations sucked out the air in front of it and stopped pumping as soon as the train had passed. Sadly for Brunel's reputation, the system was far from being a success; leathers were used to make the pistons airtight but they deteriorated badly becaue of bad weather and the effect of the salt air (some say the rats ate the grease used as a preservative) and the whole idea was abandoned on 9 September 1848. The Starcross Pumping Station still remains and, having been turned into a museum, is well worth a visit.

Penn Inn, Newton Abbot, c. 1960, in the days before the modern, traffic-light-guarded round-about arrived.

Queen Street, Newton Abbot, c. 1901.

Broadlands Post Office, Highweek Road, Newton Abbot, c. 1925.

The Avenue, Newton Abbot, c. 1908. Today the War Memorial stands where the handsome oak on the right is growing.

Courtenay Street, Newton Abbot, *c.* 1950, looking towards St Leonard's Tower. The Town Hall (centre left) is now the site of Boots. Newton Abbot's first town hall was built in 1848 (it was first known as the Vestry Room) on the site of the old poorhouse between the Devon Arms and the Dartmouth Inn at a cost of £670; permission to do away with the poorhouse had to be obtained from the Secretary of State. Magistrates began to sit there in 1850. The fittings from this Town Hall were taken to the hall seen above when it was built out of the Select Brethren's chapel.

W. Fuller & Sons, Nurserymen and Florists, at Courtenay Nursery, Newton Abbot, *c.* 1905. Today the handsome house is two council flats.

Floods in Courtenay Street, Newton Abbot, *c.* 1937.

Old view of Courtenay Street, Newton Abbot, probably of the very early nineteenth century.

Bank Street, Newton Abbot, c. 1905.

48

Newton Abbot was only just beginning to develop when the railway arrived in 1846. Its position at what was then the edge of town accounts for the many horse-drawn carriages seen here waiting for trade at the turn of the century.

Powderham Road, Newton Abbot, c. 1908.

Queen Street, Newton Abbot, c. 1924.

Courtenay Park, Newton Abbot, c. 1912.

Two

The People

An all-male outing from the Devon Arms public house in East Street, Newton Abbot, in the 1920s.

Newton Abbot Fire Brigade with its first automatic extension ladder, *c.* 1912.

Newton Abbot Fire Brigade with their fire engine, *c.* 1912. Note that they are wearing caps and have their helmets lined up on the appliance.

A fire at Bradley Mill in 1913. The medal ribbons worn by some of the members must be for the Boer War (1899–1902).

Newton Abbot Fire Brigade, 18 August 1936.

Newton Spurs Football Club, 1951–52, their first season as a South Western League team. Back, left to right: Bob Mercer, Bill Strudwick, Eric Butler, Mr Vidgeon, Mr Lawrence, Harry Butler, Charlie Smith, Jim Butler. Front: Mr Davies, Bill Anderson, Alfie Beeson, Mr McMasters, 'Wiggy' Hamley.

Newton Spurs Football Club committee, 1947–48. Back, left to right: Wilf Hooper, Walter Norrish, George Baharie, Fred Yeatman (treasurer), Mr H. Crapper (Vice-President). Front: Dick Brown, Mr Border, Jim Butler (secretary-manager), Frank Harris, Jack Brown.

Newton Spurs Football Club, 1945–46, Herald Cup finalists. Back row, left to right: Ken Pascoe, Eric Butler, Cliff Taylor, Stuart Mountford, Gordon 'Doc' Emmett, Jack Collier. Front: Ernie Prowse, Stan Watkins, Fred Stopp, Terry Waye, Vic Randall.

Newton Abbot, Courtenay Park, Bowling Green

The Bowling Green, Courtenay Park, Newton Abbot, *c.* 1923.

Newton Abbot Bowling Club was formed in 1911 at Courtenay Park, where it has played ever since. Here is the rink that were runners-up in the National Championship Rink at Wimbledon in 1954. Left to right: W. Hollow (skip), M. Morgan, L. Powlesland, G. Willingham.

Newton Abbot Bowling Club, Mid-Devon League winners, 1950. Back row, left to right: H. Northway, A. Brooking, C. Hicks, G. Boulton, A.J.W. Gillingham (capt), F. Hurst, I. Pring, W. Hopkins, H. Underhay. Front: W. Newbury, F. House, W.T. Warren (secretary), S. Powlesland (treasurer), A.J. Alves, J. Hoare.

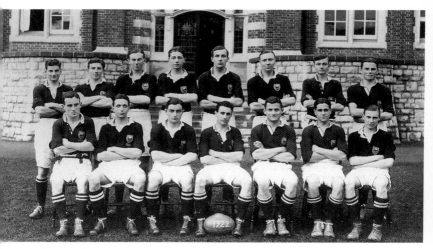

Seale Hayne College rugby 1st XV, 1922.

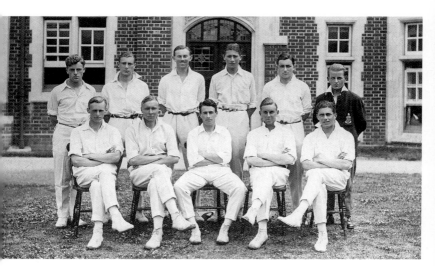

Seale Hayne cricket 1st XI, 1922. Seal Hayne is among the leading agricultural colleges in the country and is situated in fine buildings commanding superb views of both Dartmoor and the Teign estuary.

An 1866 poster on show in the Steward's Room at Newton Abbot racecourse.

Her Majesty Queen Elizabeth the Queen Mother at Newton Abbot Racecourse, when she opened the new grandstand in 1969. Her trainer Peter Cazalet is on her left, the then chairman of the racecourse, Commander Mildmay-White, on her right. The new grandstand replaced an old wooden one at the paddock which often caught fire because cigarette ends were dropped through the floor. It was such a common occurence that two firemen were stationed at the course on race days; with the erection of the new stand, however, that fireman's perk vanished.

Left: Carl Nekola, director of Newton Abbot Racecouse, claims to have done every job at the popular West Country National Hunt course except looking after the number board. He became associated with Newton Abbot racing in 1936 and was secretary there for forty years until resigning last year.

Below: Newton Abbot Racecourse, 1969, during the visit of the Queen Mother. Note the old Newton Abbot power station in the background. Racing is thought to have begun at Newton Abbot on the site of the modern course in the first half of the nineteenth century, certainly before the 1866-dated poster displayed in the Steward's Room (see p.58).

Right: The Christopher family at their Bickington, Newton Abbot, home in around 1890.

Below: General Committee for the Celebrations of HM Jubilee at Newton Abbot, 21 June 1887.

Post Office staff during the celebrations for the visit of the Duke (later George V) and Duchess of York to Newton Abbot in 1899.

Opposite above: The Devon County British Legion Women's Section rally at Newton Abbot's Recreational Ground, 1939.

Opposite below: One of many honours won at county level by the Newton Abbot British Legion Women's Section was the Standard Bearers' Competition, won by the Teign Group's standard bearer Mrs Betty Pinnegar (spelt wrongly on the certificate).

 British Legion Women's Section

DEVON COUNTY

Group Standard Bearers' Competition

This is to Certify that the

Teign Group

Standard Bearers' Competition for the year ending Sept. 30th, 19**60**

was won by *Mrs Pinnagar* of

Newton Abbot Branch

M. H. Easley County Chairman

Esfarcembe County Hon. Sec.

Left: Standard Bearers at Newton Abbot War Memorial, *c.* 1939. Left to right: -?-, Emmy Avery (County Standard Bearer), E. Coaker (Newton Abbot Standard Bearer), -?-.

Below: Newton Abbot British Legion Women's Section prepare for a supper at Legion HQ in East Street around 1958. Left to right: Mrs Minnetchon, Mrs Cleave, -?-, Mrs Avery, Mrs Jones (front), Mrs Williams, Mrs Rumbelow, Mrs Fisher, Mrs Pinn, -?-, Mrs Webb, Mrs Mills.

Remembrance Sunday at the War Memorial, Newton Abbot, 1956–57. Among the public facing the memorial in the top picture are Mrs Ethel Cleave, Percy Hunt and Bill Pinnegar, Newton Abbot British Legion branch secretary 1956–69 and subsequently its chairman. The Newton Abbot branch of the British (now Royal British) Legion was founded in 1921. The bottom picture shows the standards lowered during the the sounding of 'The Last Post'.

The Standard of the Newton Abbot branch of the Royal Naval Association being dedicated at St Leonard's church, Newton Abbot, 4 May 1957. After the service, which was conducted by the Bishop of Plymouth, the Standard was led through the town by the Royal Marine Band from Dartmouth Naval College. Roy Dolbear was Standard Bearer for twenty years, during which time he carried the Standard through many towns and cities, including Whitehall and the Festival Hall in London.

Few pictures can be found of the very early days of the Home Guard, known originally as the LDV (Local Defence Volunteers) for a short period after their formation following a radio appeal from Mr Anthony Eden in 1940. Seen here at the old Recreation Ground, Newton Abbot's first volunteers suggest Hitler would have been unwise to enter the town.

Officers of A Company, 9th Battalion, Devon Home Guard at Newton Abbot, *c.* 1943. Back row, left to right: 2nd Lts A.E. Wright, H.R. Jenkins, W.G. Westlake, G.K. Kingston, J.C. Evans, H.G. Filby. Middle: Lt L.T. Staniland, 2nd Lts R.C. King, W.J. Jones MM, J.A. Holmes, C.A. Marshall, Lt W.H. Hack, 2nd Lt L. Langmead, Lt E. Tiplady. Front: Lts H.J. Woodward, F.E. Veale MM, Capt C.E. Austin MC, Major W.C. Henly, -?-, Capt R.C.F. Whiteway-Wilkinson, Capt G. Ormrod.

Opposite above: Home Guard at the Racecourse, Newton Abbot, 1943. Major Chave was a prominent member at Newton Abbot.

Opposite below: The stand-down parade at Newton Abbot Recreation Ground of A Company, 9th Battalion, Devon Home Guard on 14 December 1944. Note the gas works in the background.

Home Guard, Anniversary, 1943.

The Commanding Officer, The 9th (Newton Abbot) Bn. Devon Home Guard, requests the honour of your attendance at the Saluting Base at the Recreation Ground, Newton Abbot on the occasion of the Anniversary Parade, Sunday, May 16th, 1943, at 4 p.m.

Please bring this card.

R.S.V.P.
  O.C. 9th (Newton Abbot) Bn. Devon H.G.
  The Drill Hall, Wolborough St. Newton Abbot.

The third anniversary of the formation of the Home Guard (Local Defence Volunteers) was marked in Newton Abbot by an Anniversary Parade at Newton Abbot Recreation Ground on 16 May 1943.

Newton Abbot Air Raid Wardens, *c.* 1942. The picture was taken on the old cricket field, which is now the car park for the new field.

The Newton Abbot Branch of the Royal Naval Association was formed in 1956 following a dinner held in Teignmouth by that town's branch. Members seen here at the time are, left to right: Reg Rendell, Betty Lewis, Ruby Rendell, Cyril Lewis (branch secretary 1956–83), Joan Rendell.

Staff from various tailors and gentlemen's outfitters in Newton Abbot on an outing to Dartmoor, *c.* 1910.

A first aid contest in the old St John Ambulance Hall around 1951. Mr J.G. George (chairman of Newton Abbot Council) and Mrs George are seated on the left; the three St John men behind the stretcher are, from left to right: -?-, Mr Hollow, John Powlesland. Others present include Stan Griggs and Ken Davey.

Lady Edwina Mountbatten, centre, with members of Newton Abbot's St John Ambulance Brigade, c. 1955. Miss K. Huddy is the nurse on the extreme left; on Lady Mountbatten's left is the Superintendent of the Ladies Division, Mrs Dorothy Paddon; the Men's Division Superintendent, Eric Kerley, is extreme right.

Mollie Pappas is seen (above) leaving for her crowning as Miss Newton Abbot at the 1951 Festival of Britain and (below) being congratulated by Mr Bickham and Councillor Joseph George (chairman of Newton Abbot Urban District Council) at the Town Hall.

Officials of the Mid-Devon Road Club, together with Councillor J.G. George (chairman Newton Abbot UDC) admiring the trophies at the Annual Dinner and Dance held at the Bradley Hotel, *c.* 1951.

Members and guests at the opening of the GWR (now British Rail) Staff Association Club (Forde Hall) on 17 May 1930. Cyril E. Lloyd, a director of the Great Western Railway (centre) performed the ceremony.

Newton Abbot's British Rail Staff Association officials and competitors outside Forde Hall during their Fur and Feather Show in 1954.

Newton Abbot British Rail Staff Association members prior to departing on an outing in the 1950s.

First camp of the Volunteer Band at Bellamarsh. Back row, left to right: Elias Gilpin, George Burns, Bill Gilpin, J. Jones, George Babbage, Col. Bearne, Bill Baker, W. Bowden. Front: Dolf Chudleigh, Harry Willcocks, Charlie Webber, J. Prout, Bob Bearne, Frank Gilpin.

Newton Abbot Salvation Army Silver Band, 1925.

Newton Abbot Young People's Singing Company, 1925. They seem a bit on the short side for male voices.

The Elsie Baker School of Dancing's production of Cinderella at the Alexandra Theatre, Newton Abbot, c. 1957. Left to right: Paulene Davey, Virginia Rose, Judith Rendell, Maureen Parnell, Fay Bartlett, T. Davey, Carole Braund, Christine Davey, Sylvia Lewis, Wendy Furze, Hilary Penn, Jacqueline Heywood.

The Newton Abbot Repertory Company
(Affiliated to the British Drama League)

Souvenir Programme

1923 1933

Dr. L. du Garde Peach
Founder and President of the Company

May 27th, 1933

Left: Newton Abbot Repertory Company programme for 27 May 1933. Dr L. du Garde was founder and President. Twenty members subscribed a guinea each to offer the council the chance to provide a platform in the Reading Room (then the Library and Lecture Room) which became the 'Little Theatre' where the company met for twenty-five years.

Below: The Repertory Company's production of Albert Casella's *Death Takes A Holiday*. Left to right: Terence Heclos, Gilbert Stead, Muriel Gardiner, Patrick Butler, Philip Rice, Sidney Monhall, George Kingston, Marion Ehlers, Grace Bradbeer.

Opposite above: The Declaration of the Poll, Newton Abbot, 26 January 1910.

Opposite below: Among the many politicans to visit Newton Abbot in post-war years was Nye Bevin, seen here at the Globe Hotel in around 1952 with Leonard Lamb (left) and Joseph George, the town's first Socialist UDC chairman.

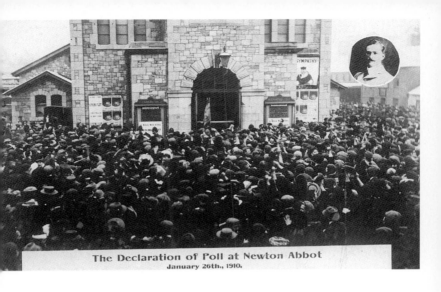

The Declaration of Poll at Newton Abbot
January 26th., 1910.

Beating the Bounds, Newton Abbot, *c.* 1901.

A shooting party including Mr Hearder, the founder-editor of the *Mid-Devon Advertiser*, and Mr Lutte, *c.* 1900.

The Coronation Service at Courtenay Park in 1953.

Just five months after her accession to the throne on 2 July 1952, Queen Elizabeth II visited Newton Abbot and is seen here passing the Drum Clock in Courtenay Street. The picture was taken from an upstairs window at the Clarendon Studio premises of local photographers Cockman and Willcocks.

Staff and directors of Pollard's Confectionery Ltd, Newton Abbot's Queen Street sweet and ice cream manufacturers, at an annual Christmas party in the old Courtenay Restaurant (now Currys) in around 1952. Among those present are Derek Pollard, Kath Pollard, Ken Pollard, Donald Pollard, Anita Palmer, Roy Leach, Joe George, Mike Meyers, Jack Terrel and Ivor Hooper. Pollard's Confectionery Ltd was founded in 1916 by Victor Pollard in Queen Street and had their factory immediately behind. Later they moved to Brunel Road. The last managing director was Derek Pollard, the business being sold in 1987 to an ice cream firm in St Blazey, Cornwall, where the name is still used under Pollard's Ice Cream.

VE Celebrations at the Penguin (now the Penn Inn), Newton Abbot. Mr Prowse is in fancy dress on the left; his brother is in drag, and a younger brother is behind Mr Matthews, who is playing the accordion.

An unknown occasion outside Newton Abbot's Town Hall, almost certainly in 1951 as it is attended by Mollie Pappas, Miss Newton Abbot for the Festival of Britain celebrations that were held that year.

Bradley Lane, Newton Abbot. The VE Day (8 May 1945) street party is being held on the former Bradley Meadows, now industrial units.

VE Day (8 May 1945) party in East Street. W. Cross's furniture lorry was used by American soldiers as a bandstand. The Fountain Hotel on the left in the picture above has since gone; the Jolly Sailor (behind Cross's lorry) remains, albeit as the Jolly Abbot.

Children from Knowles Hill, Newton Abbot, at a victory party in 1945. All the food was supplied by Newton Abbot's famous café, Madge Mellor in East Street.

St Leonard's church outing, c. 1954. The outings, always popular events, were organised for many years by Mrs Theobald of Fairfield Terrace and Mrs Venning of Stepps Meadow. Both can be seen here, along with Sydney and Dorothy Paddon, Leslie Pascoe, Valerie and Irene Rogers, Mr Melluish and his son John, and Mrs Horswell.

A wedding at St Paul's church around the later 1920s. This postcard was sold by the local photographer Mr Brooks, whose shop in Union Street is now a funeral parlour.

What appears to be an important funeral makes its way along Wolborough Street, opposite the alms house, to Totnes Road and the cemetery. The cortege has a uniformed escort who are carrying wreaths. Dated after World War One, note the early traffic sign asking drivers to 'Drive Slow Through Newton Abbot'.

Joseph 'Joe' George receives his twenty-five years Long Service Certificate as a Devon General Omnibus & Touring Company Limited driver in 1949. Born at Exmouth, he came to Newton Abbot at the age of 15 and, after working as an assistant in a local music shop, he entered service with the Devon General Company. Interesting himself in trade union affairs, he became the chairman of the Newton Abbot NUR Road Transport Branch, of which he was a founder member and chairman for fifteen years. He was first returned to the Urban District Council as Labour Party member for Bradley Ward in 1946 and within five years was elected as its first Labour chairman. Among his many civic interests, a principal one was road safety, and it was in that area that he arranged many cycling proficiency tests for schoolchildren. His death at the age of 55 in 1957 was a great blow to the town. His wife Evelyn (see opposite), who still lives in Newton Abbot and is aged 88, was a bus conductress for thirty years.

Right: Mrs Evelyn George, wife of Joseph George (see opposite), was employed as a bus conductress from 1943 to 1973.

Below: Members of the local Devon General Bus Company workforce at a function in 1951. Among those present are Bert Tucker, Tim Dawson, Ernie Lawrence, Joe George and Albert George.

Mostly members of the Cross family on an outing to a now-unknown destination in around 1921. The family had been in business as furniture removers and salesmen since around 1910 in Market Square and later had premises in Queen Street and at 10 East Street. They moved to their present home in the old Cottage Hospital at 36 East Street in 1921, purchasing the building for £2,750. Among those seen here are Mrs Cross, Sydney Paddon (centre), Dorothy Paddon on his left, Bert Paddon, Mrs Irene Rodgers and the local cobbler, Mr George Ford.

Opposite above: Skating on Stover Lake, Newton Abbot, 1892.

Opposite below: Francis Watts (1849–1929) was a partner at Baker, Watts, Alsop & Woollcombe from 1880 to 1929. Today the firm is known as Woollcombe, Beer, Watts. It was founded in 1831, moving into its present offices in the old Congregational (later United Reform) church in Queen Street in 1986, the building being officially opened on 6 May 1988 by Revd John Huxtable DD, and His Honour Judge A.C. Goddard MC, DL. The church was used as such from 1876 to 1984.

Bearnes' School, Newton Abbot, c. 1904.

Group II, Wolborough Council School, c. 1912.

Miss Tozer (at the back) and her class at the Wolborough Church of England Primary School in Union Street, Newton Abbot around 1936.

A party of Newton Abbot ladies about to set off on an outing in around 1912 with the driver (cigarette in mouth) looking singularly unconcerned at the prospect of such charming company all to himself. The Tea Rooms in the background were at the corner of Wolborough Street and East Street. They later became popular as Ye Olde Bunne Shoppe, and today are the home of Leslie Fulford, the estate agent.

A dance at the Globe Hotel, 1952. Among those present are: Christiana Hodge, Mrs Evelyn George, Mrs Tookey, Mr Tookey (councillor), -?-, -?-, Mr A.J. Hodge (councillor), -?-, -?-, Mr Joseph George (council chairman).

Outside the VAD Hospital, Newton Abbot, 8 July 1918. Back row, left to right: Sgt Flenkmen (Devonshire Regt), Ella Kenshole (VAD), -?-, -?-, Pte A. Venn (Bedford Regt). Front row includes: Cpl Wellis (Royal Welsh Fusiliers), Pte J. Ash (Berks), Signalman N. Audron (2nd Bat. MGC), Pte H. Strutt (2nd DL).

Prince George (Duke of Kent) lays a wreath at the War Memorial in Market Square during his visit to Newton Abbot on 25 June 1931.

St Leonard's church Harvest Supper. The flags and the banner 'Congratulations ER' suggest this is 1953.

Walter Cross with his new Ford car outside 36 East Street, Newton Abbot, his furniture removal business premises in about 1924, with his daughters Daphne (left) and Irene.

The 4th Newton Abbot cub pack, c. 1950. The pack was formed in 1927 and met in its present HQ in Wolborough Street.

The 4th Newton Abbot scout and cub group, c. 1950. The three scouters at centre of sitting row are, left to right: -?-, Scoutmaster Bob Howe, Cub Master, Mr Coleman. The cub third from the left in the third row back, Peter Jackson, had a great-great-uncle who served at Mafeking under Lord Baden-Powell, who formed the Scout Movement (1907).

Three

At Work

A lorry belonging to W. Cross & Co, the well-known Newton Abbot furnishers, *c.* 1913.

The railway station, Newton Abbot. Addressed to an RCAF Corporal at Down Ampney near Cirencester, this postcard dates from around the end of World War One.

A south-bound train leaves Newton Abbot station in the late 1930s. Station Cottages on the right were bombed on the night of 4 August 1940 and a total of fifteen people were killed. The well-known West Country publishers David & Charles (now Reader's Digest) later occupied the site.

Newton Abbot station decorated for the visit of Queen Elizabeth II on 2 July 1952.

The 'Newtonian' coach, which met most trains at the turn of the century and was also used for popular trips across Dartmoor.

The summing-up

These facts tell an eloquent story of the grand concerted effort made at the Western Garage. In the centre pages, you see some shots of the works and of the folk who made these figures possible.

Aircraft Components Repaired

SPITFIRE AND SEAFIRE :	
Main Planes	662
BEAUFIGHTER AND BEAUFORT	
Main Planes	167
BEAUFIGHTER :	
Stern Groups	216
BEAUFIGHTER :	
Rudders	769
SPITFIRE :	
Rudders, Elevators, Flaps and Tail Planes	3,840

Tribute

We salute, with pride, those members of the Western Garage personnel who, at home and abroad, on land, on sea and in the air, served their country nobly and well. Older men and young apprentices alike, they worthily upheld the great British traditions. Let us also pay tribute to those who have fallen . . . honouring their memory while giving thanks for Victory.

The old Western Garage in Wolborough Street and Engineering Works Ltd played an important part in Newton Abbot's war effort. In 1940 essential work on parts of the Bomb Projector, the method of protection employed by fishing vessels and coastal steamers against German dive bombers, was carried out there. In October 1942 the garage closed completely, being taken over by the Civilian Repair Organisation, RAF. Some 300 people, almost half of them women, were employed on repairing firstly smaller components, rudders, tailplanes, elevators, etc. So skilful did the workforce become that they soon graduated to repairing the complete main planes, mostly Spitfires but also Beaufighters. After the war Western Garage manufactured tyres and batteries; today it is the site of a car park.

Western Garage, 48–56 Wolborough Street, Newton Abbot, c. 1946. The garage stood opposite St Leonard's church.

Beaufighter rudders being repaired by Civilian Repair Organisation, RAF, at Western Garage, Wolborough Street, during World War Two.

Left: Workers at the Civilian Repair Organisation at Western Garage.

Below: Spitfire fighter main planes being repaired at the Bradley Lane factory, Newton Abbot, during World War Two.

Erecting a lamp post outside the Bradley Inn (now the Jolly Farmer) in Market Street, *c.* 1905. Old photographs often contain crowds of children, sometimes specially collected for the purpose by the photographer; here a passing postman finds time off from his rounds to help with the crowd scene.

Decon Clay Works, Newton Abbot, c. 1925. Bert Hooper, on right in the top picture, the landlord of the nearby Passage House Inn (see p.136), worked here as a clay cutter, part of which job included pushing the loaded waggons seen here along the rails to the quay at Hackney Canal. The clay, the deposits of which had been worked for hundreds of years, is said to have been transported by barge down the River Teign in 'lumps' or loose form.

Workers at the Decon Clay Works, c. 1925. Of interest here are the tools being used by the workmen. The man on the extreme right is holding a tubil, a single-bladed mattock-type tool which was used to lift the pre-cut lump of clay from the ground; a poge, held by the third man from the right, carried the lumps to the waggon.

Ivor Bassett with a modern cutter-loader machine in a modern adit clay mine, *c.* 1966.

A Shaft at West Golds Quarry in the 1930s. It was here in 1951 that the old Devon & Courtenay Clay Company first introduced the steel arches (see above), used in conjunction with a timber lining, that took the place of old heavy timbering.

Clay cellars at Teignbridge on the Stover Canal, c. 1914.

The steam tug *Kestrel*, operated by WWB out of the wharf at Jetty Marsh in Newton Abbot, and used to haul clay barges down the Stover Canal to the Teign estuary and on to Teignmouth. Arriving before World War One, she replaced the old sailing vessels that used to ply the estuary with their square-rigged and high sails, looking very much like Viking ships. The *Kestrel*, powered by a Kelvin paraffin engine and seen here in the early 1920s, was later joined by a sister boat, the *Heron*. Competition by road transport led to the *Kestrel* being scrapped not long before World War Two; the *Heron* is said to have gone to Dunkirk (1940) and never returned.

Charles Blake (left) was the son of Edward Blake, the moving spirit in the Devon & Courtenay Clay Co. He had entered the trade at the age of nineteen as sales representative in Stoke-on-Trent. He became an original partner in Watts, Blake, Bearne & Co. (today's WBB Devon Clays Ltd) in 1860. It was due to his efforts on the sales side that the company urgently needed more clay land, the firm taking up new leases on the Clifford, Watts, Templer and Swete estates. He is seen here with his old friend Charles Green, who became engineering advisor to WBB. A considerable believer in water power, Green numbered the early hydro-power installation at Lynmouth among his many West Country achievments.

An early adit-type mine at Newton Abbot in the 1920s.

Men cutting clay 'balls' by hand at one of the many timbered square pits around Newton Abbot, c. 1921. Although referred to as clay 'balls', the clay was cut out in rectangular blocks, a process which lead to the sides of the pit looking as if they were built of blocks or bricks (as here). The block became oval as it was 'knocked around' in the various stages of its transportation, and it was at this stage that it became known as a ball.

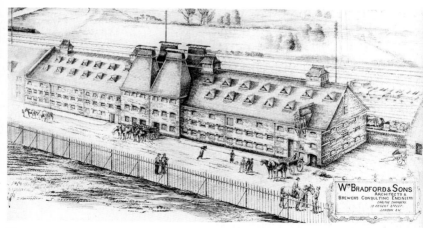

The architects drawings for the new building at Tuckers Maltings at Quay Road, Newton Abbot in 1900. Much of the area in the front has long since been developed, but part of it remains open as Osborne Park. As Quay Road suggests, the site was chosen because of the proximity of the local canal and River Teign. The arrival of the railway station just around the corner a few years later was a fortunate coincidence.

Edwin Tucker founded a seed merchant business at Ashburton in 1831, which remains today one of the oldest surviving independent agricultural companies in Britain. With their contacts and knowledge of the agricultural community, the firm opened a malting business at Newton Abbot, which was rebuilt in 1900 (see opposite) and has been considerably extended over the years.

Original (1900) machinery still in use at Tucker's Maltings.

Left: John Parnell Tucker (1865–1936).

Below: Tankers capable of carrying 1,800 gallons of cyder lined up at Whiteway's cyder works at Newton Abbot in 1951.

Mr Simmons's waggon delivering coal in Abbotsbury Road in around 1928.

A Foden steam lorry belonging to the Frank White fleet (see p.115).

Mr W.G. Carnell with his haulier's lorry outside the Market House Inn, c. 1913.

Laying electricity cables outside the Sun Inn in East Street, around early 1920s.

Although the railways had taken over much of the business from the carriers who plodded by horse along routes which criss-crossed Devon in all directions, there was still a need to get the goods out to the many communities away from the train. The horse-drawn carrier existed into the 1920s in many places before being replaced by a different kind of horse power. Frank White was one of Newton Abbot's earlier such conversions and is seen here in around 1920. Given the pristine condition of the lorry, and the Foden Steam Waggon premises behind, it is possible that he has just taken delivery of a new lorry.

F.C. Heywood, the Highweek Street Dairy, with their first motor delivery van in around 1910. Later the premises became Field & Sons, still a dairy, and today it is the Post Office Sorting Office.

W. Cross & Son's canvas-roofed Ford lorry outside the East Street premises they had just purchased (Paige's name is still above the door) in around 1922. The lorry was commandeered by the authorities during World War Two and used as an ambulance. In 1941, during a bombing raid, it became jammed under the railway arch in Quay Road.

Right: J. Gibbons & Sons Ltd, Newton Abbot's Market Street grocers, enjoyed a fine reputation when this advertisement appeared in the local bus service timetable in 1958.

Below: E.F. Huxtable, Queen Street, Newton Abbot, 1910. One of the town's oldest firms, Huxtable had been in Queen Street since 1860.

QUEEN'S HOTEL

Family and Commercial

NEWTON ABBOT

FULLY LICENSED

FACING B.R. STATION

The situation of this hotel makes it an
ideal centre for Dartmoor and all
resorts on the South Devon Coast

32 ROOMS WITH HOT AND COLD WATER

GARAGE

Phone : Visitors 496, Office 216

QUEEN'S HOTEL (NEWTON ABBOT) LTD.

Managing Director : **A. E. WYATT**

Queen's Hotel, on the corner of Queen Street and Courtenay Park Road, was, and still
is, one of Newton Abbot's best-known hotels. Advertised here in the *Newton Abbot
Coronation Year* (1953) Guide, the hotel is opposite the railway station.

Good Food means Good Health . . .

obtain your

Groceries and Provisions

from

SLADES
5 BANK STREET, NEWTON ABBOT
Telephone 1827-8

(opposite the Post Office)

and be SURE of getting the Best

Weekly Deliveries in Town and Country Districts

Established in Devon in 1837

- always look for SLADES -

SHOPS ALSO IN ASHBURTON, BOVEY TRACEY, TORQUAY

Right: Like the picture on page 117, this advertisement is from Newton Abbot's 1958 Bus Service Timetable. Note the old-style 'No Waiting' signs then in use.

Below: Ross & Co, wine merchants at 28 Queen Street, Newton Abbot, made their own soda water in a factory at the rear of these premises.

Telegrams:
"Ross, Newton Abbot."

Telephone 2 Y 3.

ROSS & CO.

WINE & SPIRIT MERCHANTS.

Ross' Wines & Spirits
THE OLDEST AND BEST.

ROSS' Dry Ginger Ale, Soda Water, &c.

Of all Dealers, or Rail Carriage Paid ex NEWTON ABBOT.

EXPERT ALE & STOUT BOTTLERS

Office, Stores and Factory: 28, Queen Street, NEWTON ABBOT.

J. Potter & Sons Ltd's Tor Garage, Hay Tor, Newton Abbot, c. 1956.

This picture of Jimmy Steere's cycle shop in Wolborough Street was almost certainly taken during World War One. Jimmy was one of the town's characters and is especially known for his one-man-band performances. He is seen here second from left.

Mortimer Bros' Printing Works, Lemon Place, Newton Abbot, *c.* 1905, with members of the staff outside the composing room.

Harvey's drapers shop and undertakers, Bank Street, Newton Abbot, *c.* 1905. Harvey's have used this card as an advertisement to tell their customers (on the reverse) that they have a 'Special Show For This Week – See Windows and Note our Cash Prices'.

Cecil Ford, the Wolborough Street, Newton Abbot, butcher, c. 1954. Today the premises are occupied by Court's furnishers.

Newton Abbot railway station, c. 1903. When it was first proposed to take the railway south from Exeter to Plymouth, a decision had to be made as to whether it should follow its present line or go across country via Ashburton. In order to see which route would provide the most custom, road traffic at both Ashburton and Newton Abbot was counted for a three-week period, men being stationed in the latter town for the purpose at St Leonard's Tower. It is said that when the good people of Ashburton realised the reason for the count they ran cabs out of the town and back again to increase their figures, free rides going to all and sundry. But Newton Abbot still exceeded them in traffic volume. The railway line reached Newton Abbot towards the end of 1846. Originally Newton Abbot had two stations, but neither was more than a collection of tumble-down and temporary sheds. The up-line was served from close to the Railway Hotel; the down-platform was more or less where the present station (which soon replaced both) now is.

Opposite below: Queen Street, Newton Abbot, c. 1960. John Balster, of Balster & Son, the grocers shop in the centre, still ran his shop in the old fashioned manner, weighing most things out by hand and keeping the various goods in tins.

T. J. GIBBINS,

76 Queen Street, *NEWTON ABBOT.*

For everything that is

NEW AND
UP-TO-DATE

in . .

Millinery

and . .

General Drapery.

AT LONDON
STORE PRICES.

T.J. Gibbins, milliners and general drapers at 76 Queen Street, Newton Abbot, as seen in the *Mid-Devon Times* handbook of *Newton Abbot and Its History and Development* by A.J. Rhodes, which was printed at the *Mid-Devon & Newton Times* offices at 66 Queen Street. The paper, which cost one penny at the time, was published on Saturdays. S. Wooton (below) was a well-known printer, stationer, bookbinder and newsagent found at 22–24 Courtenay Street.

22 & 24, COURTENAY STREET, NEWTON ABBOT.

DIE SINKER
. and .
RELIEF STAMPER.

—o—

COPPER PLATE
ENGRAVER
AND PRINTER.

—o—

IMPORTER OF
FANCY GOODS.

S. WOTTON,

TOYS & GAMES.

Printer, . .
Stationer, Bookbinder,
Newsagent, &c., . . .

22 & 24, COURTENAY STREET, NEWTON ABBOT.

Right: The Regent Restaurant & Hygienic Bakery, 9 Regent Street, Newton Abbot, *c.* 1902.

Below: John Harley, goldsmith and jeweller, Courtenay Street, Newton Abbot, *c.* 1898.

Visitors to Teignmouth will find the

Regent Restaurant & Hygienic Bakery

AT 9, REGENT STREET.

Central, Commodious, and Up-to-date. — Hot and Cold Luncheons.
Chops, Steaks, Soups, and Ices. — Wines, Ales, &c.

BRANCH:—11, FORE STREET, TEIGNMOUTH.

W. H. BONNER, Proprietor.

Latest Novelties in Gold and Fancy Jewellery.
Silver Toilet Requisities, Knick Knacks, &c., &c.,
suitable for Presents.

20 **JOHN HARLEY** 20

GOLDSMITH SILVERSMITH

H. Norris] [Newton Abbot.

John Harley, Goldsmith and Jeweller. COURTENAY ST., NEWTON ABBOT.

Watches, Clocks, Silver, and Electro Plate,
OPTICS, BAROMETERS, &c., &c.,
&c. In the Newest Designs, at popular prices.

Aerial view of the old Newton Abbot power station in 1945, when the cooling tower was still wearing its wartime camouflage of painted buildings that were supposed to hide it from the Luftwaffe. Originally it was planned to build two such towers but finances dictated otherwise, Newton Abbot's best-known landmark arriving in 1940. It was demolished by explosives in 1974.

Aerial view of Newton Abbot's old gas works that fronted on to The Avenue. The football field is immediately behind, the old cricket field beyond that again. Taken around 1948, the picture gives a good view of the canal (front). The area around the chimney in the centre is now occupied by Renwicks' Cars and the headquarters of both the fire service and St John Ambulance Brigade.

Vicary's wool and leather works at Bradley Mill, *c.* 1938. Founded in 1747, Vicary's works expanded, continuing in the process of gillmongering and wool combing. They were under contract to the Admiralty and the War Office during World War One. The business closed in 1972.

Newton Abbot, Cottage Hospital

The Cottage Hospital, Newton Abbot, *c.* 1905. An extension was opened by the Prince of Wales (later Edward VIII) in 1927.

Staff of the Newton Abbot Co-operative Bakery in King Street, *c.* 1910.

The Newton Abbot Co-operative Bakery, King Street, Newton Abbot, *c.* 1912. The head baker, Alfred W. Prudence, is second from the right.

Henry P. Warner ironmongers shop in
Bank Street, Newton Abbot, as advertised in
around 1903.

G.A. Barnes, London Drug Stores, 14
Courtenay Street, Newton Abbot, *c.* 1900.

THE NEWTON ABBOT
Co-operative Society Ltd.

Central Premises
17-23 QUEEN STREET
Tel. 791-2

We serve all parts of the District

BRANCHES AT:

Abbotskerswell · Bank Street · Bovey Tracey
Chudleigh Knighton · Decoy · Ipplepen · Kingskerswell
Kingsteignton · Lustleigh · Moretonhampstead

SHOP AT THE CO-OP..

Left: The Newton Abbot Co-operative Society's headquarters in Queen Street in 1950.

Below: Newton Abbot Market, c. 1952.

THE MARKET, NEWTON ABBOT

C.J. Dimond & Son.

Established 1893

**FURNITURE REMOVALS ANY DISTANCE
STORAGE, PACKING AND SHIPPING**

Expert Service and Modern Equipment

**VICTORIA RD,
TORQUAY**

Tel.: Torquay 4804
(3 lines)

Warehouses:
VICTORIA ROAD, ALEXANDRA ROAD, ALEXANDRA LANE
And at BRIXHAM

INCORPORATING *Bakers* ERDINGTON
BIRMINGHAM
Tel.: Erdington 2644 & 0315

C.J. Dimond & Son of Victoria Lane, Newton Abbot, from a 1951 town directory.

Telephone 55.

A. A. PHILLIPS,

High-Class Baker,
Confectioner, Caterer, &c.

68, Queen Street, NEWTON ABBOT.

Afternoon
Tea Cakes—
a large
assortment.

□

Wedding
Cakes,
a Speciality.

□

Large
Dining Rooms.

A.A. Phillips, 68 Queen Street, Newton Abbot, 1912.

EASE! COMFORT! HEALTH!

Why walk in pain, when STILING'S

INFALLIBLE CORN CURE

Will remove your CORNS in a few days?

This preparation is, without doubt, the most successful yet introduced for the painless removal of both hard and soft **CORNS, BUNIONS,** and **Hardened** and **Thickened Skin,** by whatever cause produced.

In Bottles, 7½d. & 1/1½; free by post for 9 or 15 Stamps.

Prepared only by

JOHN EDWARD STILING, Dispensing Chemist,
(From JOHN BELL & Co., 225, Oxford Street, London.)
4, Courtenay Street (opposite Bank Street), **NEWTON ABBOT.**

John Edward Stiling, the Courtenay Street chemist, may not have had a cure for everything. But his 'Infallible Corn Cure', even if it might not get past today's more stringent advertising standards, would 'remove your corns in a few days' – his words, in a 1912 advert, not ours! Today the premises are part of Austin's department store.

J. Webber & Son, 10 Courtenay Street, Newton Abbot. Back in 1912, when this advertisement appeared in Devonshire, Past and Present, By Pen & Camera, sports shops stocked mainly fishing and shooting items. It is a sign of the times for the working classes that today football, cricket, rugby, hockey, etc. probably lead the way in our leisure-oriented society.

THE MID-DEVON SPORTS DEPÔT.

J. WEBBER & SONS
FISHING TACKLE SPORTING GOODS.

Fishing Tackle,
Guns, Rifles,
AND ALL
Sporting Goods.

J. Webber & Sons
10, Courtenay St.,
NEWTON ABBOT
(and at EXETER).

Mr and Mrs Ashworth and their staff at the Madge Mellor café they founded in East Street, Newton Abbot, in 1928. Seen here in the 1930s, the back row includes: Miss Florence, Miss Ridgeway, Miss Howe, Percy Penge, Len Pocock, Miss Gray, Miss Carnall, Mrs Howard. Front row includes: Miss Wintoe, Miss Rene Webber, Sarah Ashworth, Robert Sydney Ashworth, Freda Symonds, Ivy Webber, Miss Faulkener.

Madge Mellor Café, Queen Street, Newton Abbot, *c.* 1955.

Inside at Madge Mellor, where the specialities included delicious hand-raised pies and dairy cream (real Devonshire as well) cakes.

Four

The Villages

The Church School (left) and Jubilee Memorial drinking fountain, Kingsteignton, *c.* 1918. The fountain, barely visible in the background, was unveiled by Lord Clifford in 1887. It had to make way for modern traffic requirements and was moved to the gardens. The old Co-op shop is centre left; the toilets in the centre background were once a garage.

The Passage House Inn, Hackney, Kingsteignton. This ancient inn, seen above in around 1894 with the landlord, Bert Hooper, sitting second from the left, was much used then by local clay workers and bargees from the nearby Hackney Canal. With a few cottages, it once formed the tiny hamlet of Hackney, whose water supply was a small well near the bridge that took the railway line across the marshes. The families living in the cottages had to fetch their water by boat! The Hackney Canal, opened in 1843, ran for around half a mile from Hackney to the Newton Abbot road and was used to carry clay. The canal finally closed in 1928, by which time the cottages were mostly empty. All fell into disrepair but some ruins can still be seen. Today, only the inn, which has moved up-market, and the nearby Passage House Hotel remain. The bottom picture is dated around 1950.

Fore Street, Kingsteignton, c. 1904. Eddle's grocery shop became a sweet shop but is now empty. Also closed is the shop (later Abrahams) to the left of Eddles. The thatched house on the right stood in front of Honeywill's slaughterhouse; today it is Hill's Garage.

Fore Street, Kingsteignton, c. 1904. Mrs Pickett's paper shop on the right is still a paper shop. The earliest reference to the village is in the Anglo-Saxon Chronicle, where it appears as Tegntum ('farm on the Teign'). The 'Kings' derives from the town's being part of the the king's demesne. Domesday tells us that 'The King has a manor called Teintona which King Edward (the Confessor) held on the day he was alive and dead.' Domesday treated Harold II as if he never existed.

Fore Street, Kingsteignton, *c.* 1905, with the Bell Inn on the left.

The Bell Inn, Kingsteignton, *c.* 1909. Ward's butchers van is on the right.

Fore Street, Kingsteignton, *c.* 1909.

The lovely named Dew Drop Inn (extreme right), Kingsteignton, *c.* 1906. Berry Farm is next to it, with Vallance's wheelwrights on the left.

Gestridge Road Cottages, Kingsteignton, *c.* 1900.

Crossley Moor Road, Kingsteignton, *c.* 1905. The village is well known for its centuries old 'Ram Roasting' ceromony on Whit Monday. Legend has it that the sacrifice of a ram ended a lengthy drought at Whitsuntide, a spring issuing from Rydon. It still flows through the village and past the church.

St Michael's church, Kingsteignton, *c.* 1905. The cottages on the left, like so much of the village's thatch, have been demolished. Today, only the south porch and the adjoining part of the aisle remain of the church which was rebuilt in 1318, most of the rest of the building being from the fifteenth century, including the handsome red sandstone and limestone tower, which dates from 1480.

Exeter Road, Kingsteignton, *c.* 1909. Heathman's grocery shop, later Staddon's, is now a washerette.

York and Wollaton Terraces, Exeter Road, Kingsteignton, *c.* 1914. Farley's coal waggon is making deliveries.

Exeter Road, Kingsteignton, *c.* 1906.

The Kings Arms, Kingsteignton, c. 1925.

Gestridge Road, Kingsteignton, c. 1949. Bartlett's shop on the corner, once the home of Kingsteignton Co-operative Society, is now a private house.

A horse-drawn bus outside the Kings Arms Hotel, Kingsteignton, c. 1898. Although advertising on public transport was far from universal at the time, Whites (see p.115) have grasped its potential.

Crossley Moor Road, Kingsteignton, c. 1905.

In 1938 a high tide around noon (this picture was taken two hours earlier) pushed the River Teign back and caused it to burst its banks near the racecourse. The floods stopped traffic until the following day. The Broadclyst–Exeter–Teignmouth–Torquay bus seen here was one of the last vehicles to brave the waters.

The reverse of this postcard showing the floods in Kingsteignton Road in 1938 tells us that 'these two men are asking for trouble . . . it is an early photograph in the brick works where [the water] was up to the horses' mangers . . . the Co-op delivered bread here on horseback'.

Kingsteignton, c. 1930. Although white lines have appeared, the motor car is still very conspicous by its absence here. Today there is a roundabout by the lamppost-cum-signpost and the drinking trough.

Abbotskerswell Football Club, 1904. With the Victorian concept of muscular Christianity still very much in vogue, it is not surprising to find the vicar posing with the team. Back row, left to right: F. Manning, G. Webber, Fred Norton, W. Manning. Middle: G. Cowell, W. Brooks, J. Coombes, Revd F.G. Campbell, G. Maddicott. Front: W. Crook, W. Honeywill, J. Norton. In keeping with many old football pictures, boy-scout-type shorts (and belts) are worn by the players.

Abbotskerswell Cricket Club, 1902. Back row, left to right: C. Hawkins, V. Herring, A. Wood, W. Manning, G. Webber, F. Howard, W. Prowse. Middle: F. Lee, G. Cowell, G. Hart, A. Hawkins, G. Elliott. Front: H. Smith, Fred Norton, W. Brooks, A. Howard. There has to be a reason for Fred Norton being the only player to be given a Christian name because he is again given that honour in the football picture opposite, where he seems to have grown a moustache.

Kingskerswell Cricket Club, 1958. Back row, left to right: A.D. Cheesman (secretary), J. Hawkins, D. Woollacott, J. Ridgeway, N.F. Roberts, G. Kidd, J. Vanstone, D. Luscombe, R.W. Fraser (chairman). Front: D. Sharples, N. Fone, E. Fone (captain), L. Evans, I. Evans.

Vicarage Corner, Kingskerswell, *c.* 1902.

Ye Olde Whitpot Mill, Kingskerswell, *c.* 1929.

Right: Aller-Vale Garage, Newton Road,
Kingskerswell, 1950.

Below: Fore Street, Kingskerswell, c. 1905. The
house on the corner with Daccabridge Road is
now the village hairdressers shop.

Trott's Hotel, Kingskerswell, *c.* 1900.

The Lord Nelson Hotel, Kingskerswell, *c.* 1925. The village's name means 'the well where cress grows'. The 'Kings' came later and signifies that the manor belongs to the Crown; nearby Abbotskerswell belonged to the Abbot (of Horton, Dorset), who owned the manor at the time of Domesday.

An unidentified Kingskerswell outing to an unknown (usually Dartmoor) destination in the middle 1920s. Note the 12 mph limit imposed on charabancs at this time, which meant all-day journeys over bumpy roads to distant attractions such as Exmoor and Cheddar.

The Seven Stars, Kingskerswell, c. 1914.

The old bridge which took Kingskerswell's Fore Street over the busy A380 Torquay main road and has since been replaced by a more modern bridge.

Combeinteignhead Village Hall. Seen here in the 1930s, the much used hall is also much altered.

Combeinteignhead Post Office, c. 1905.

Stokeinteignhead Football Club, 1950. Back row, left to right: Frank Melhuish, Dennis Balkwill, P. Rigg, Dick Lock, Ted Smith, Ernie Baker. Front: Roy Lock, Chris Prowse, Fred Melhuish, Jim Curtis, Den Woodley.

The Church House Inn, Stokeinteignhead, *c.* 1953. Left to right: Bill Noel, Fred Riggs (landlord), Mrs Hill, Mrs Middleton.

Stokeinteignhead Post Office, *c.* 1920, looking towards Newton Abbot. The post office has since moved to the opposite side of the road.

Consecration of the new Burial Ground at Stokeinteignhead, 27 June 1912.

Stokeinteignhead, c. 1905. Even today the village, happily escaping the heavy hand of the developer, retains much of its idyllic Edwardian air, the area around the post office, the Church House Inn and St Andrew's church being especially attractive. The church is fourteenth-century with fifteenth-century enlargements; subsequent restorations failed to do any damage.

A party in Stokeinteignhead Village Hall (demolished in the 1950s). Among those enjoying themselves are Dick Lock, Susie Lee, Iris Prowse, 'Gran' Stevens, June Osmond, Rose Jarvis and Pam Lock.

Another Stokeinteignhead party. This one was in 1951 and on view are Thelma Prideaux, Doris Melhuish, George Calver, Jean Proswe, Paulene Wall and Bob Robins.

Stokeinteignhead villagers pose before leaving on an outing to a now unknown destination around 1925. Ball Ltd of Newton Abbot supplied the charabanc.

Threshing at Stokeinteignhead, c. 1939. The workers include Fred Pook, Bill French, Bari Blencoe (and his dog Dina), and Pam and Pauline Wall.

Stokeinteignhead Home Guard, c. 1943. Among those pictured here are Henry Lock, Bernard Brimmicombe, Frank Dyer, Dick Lock, Cliff Brimmicombe, Den Balkwill and Denzil Lock.

George Martin, of Stokeinteignhead, with his daughters Louise (later Mrs Vranch) and Evelyn (later Mrs Martin) in 1904.

Stokeinteignhead School Maypole Dancers, 1928. Back row, left to right: -?-, Geoff Dunn, Reg Prowse, Morgan. Middle: Chris Prowse, Joyce Bowhay, Harry Clark, Freda Lock, -?-, Dick Dyer, Win Robins, Cyril Greenaway, Bettey Bearne. Front: Reg Greenaway, Loveday Clark, Lena Loud, Olive Moery, Cyril Pratt, Ivy Perkins, Norma Hartland.

Stokeinteignhead School, c. 1927. Back row, left to right: Olive Morey, Dorothy Phillips, -?-, Bill Callard, Art Rowe, Richards, Roy Prowse. Second row: Bob Lear, Ivy Perkins, Queenie Stoneman, Win Robins, Rose Robins, Kathleen Northcott, -?-, Maud Loud, White. Third row: Cyril Greenaway, Cyril Pratt, Lena Loud, Emma Jane Sarahs, Margery Phillips, Freda Lock, Beate Beare, Eddie Skinner, Dick Dyer. Front: Henry Loud, Reg Prowse, Cyril Hodge, Reg Greenaway, Harry Clark, Geoff Dunn, Chris Prowse, Joe Robins.

Acknowledgements

We are deep in debt to the Town & Great Western Railway Museum in St Paul's Road for kind permission to include much of their pictorial material in this book. And especially to Felicity Cole, for her excellent introduction and encouragement, and Christiana Ditchburn, whose encouragement included many practical cups of tea. Also to Tony Paddon for access to his outstanding collection of old Newton Abbot photographs and for his wealth of information on the town. The love of all three for the place and its past was so evident. We never cease to be astonished at the trust and welcome people show when they allow us to borrow their treasured pictures. But it is not really surprising, is it? Like ourselves, they have a love for the past and are usually only too happy to share that love – and their pictures – with others.

So many have generously allowed us to use their own material and we must thank them all:

Neil Ashworth, Bob Benson of Newton Abbot Bowling Club, Tony Bowhay, Steve Carreck of the WBB Devon Clay Company, Evelyn George, Ted Gosling, Mark Hayman of Newton Spurs FC, Arthur Jackson, Chris Jones, Betty Lewis, Bert Mitchell, Marjory Mulrooney of Woollcombe Beer Watts, Carl Nekola, Bill and Mary Pinnegar, Donald Pollard, Phil Riggs, Mollie Thomas, Joanna Webber of Tucker's Maltings, Alan Wiktorko and Ron Williams.